ANCIENT WORLDS

MIRANDA SMITH AND PHILIP STEELE

KINGFISHER

First published 2016 by Kingfisher
an imprint of Macmillan Children's Books
20 New Wharf Road, London N1 9RR
Associated companies throughout the world
www.panmacmillan.com

Consultants: Margaret Maitland; Dr Hugh Bowden, Kings College London

Illustrations by: Roger Stuart, Steve Weston, Gary Hanna,
Peter Bull Art Studio, Steve Stone (represented by Artist Partners Ltd),
Thomas Bayley and Kevin Jones Associates

Design by White-Thompson Publishing Ltd www.wtpub.co.uk
Tall Tree Ltd www.talltreebooks.co.uk

ISBN 978-0-7534-3853-4

Copyright © Macmillan Publishers International Ltd 2016

9 8 7 6 5 4 3 2
2TR/0516/WKT/UG/128MA

A CIP catalogue record for this book is available from the British Library.

Printed in China

Note to readers: The website addresses listed in this book are correct at the time of publishing.
However, due to the ever-changing nature of the Internet, website addresses and content can change.
Websites can contain links that are unsuitable for children. The publisher cannot be held responsible for
changes in website addresses or content, or for information obtained through third-party websites.
We strongly advise that Internet searches should be supervised by an adult.

The Publisher would like to thank the following for permission to reproduce their material. Every care has been taken to trace copyright holders.
(t = top, b = bottom, c = centre, r = right, l = left):
Cover c Shutterstock/AISA – Everett; Front & Back cover background Shutterstock/leoks; Back cover l Shutterstock/Andre Nantel; bc Shutterstock/WitR; r Shutterstock/Kamira; pages 1 Shutterstock/dkART;
5 Shutterstock/moonfish8; 6bl Shutterstock/Jose Ignacio Soto; 6tr AKG/Erich Lessing; 7bl Alamy/Tor Eigeland; 7bc Shutterstock/Carlos Arguelles; 7tr Bridgeman Art Library/Giraudon; 8tr Shutterstock/
BOSKO; 8 British Museum (EA 9999); 9 British Museum Harris Papyrus(EA 9999 (same) 8-9 background Shutterstock/Maugli; 9tl Art Archive/Dagli Orti; 9tr Art Archive/Musee du Louvre/Dagli Orti;
10br Art Archive/Dagli Orti; 11tr Shutterstock/Maugli; 11bc Bridgeman Art Library/Louvre Musee; 11br British Museum (EA 59334); 12–13 Shutterstock/AISA – Everett; 12br British Museum; 13bl British
Museum (GR 1888); 13br British Museum (EA 1242); 14l British Museum (EA 15671); 14r British Museum; 15 British Museum (GR 1894, 1101.269); 17tr British Museum (EA 6046 &others); 17 British
Museum (EA 41187); 17 University College London, Petrie Museum of Egyptian Archaeology (UC63042); 18–19 Corbis/Yann Arthus-Bertrand; 18cr AKG/Boston Museum of Fine Arts; 19tc Art Archive/
Egyptian Museum, Cairo/Dagli Orti; 19cl AKG/Feuardet Collection; 19cr Shutterstock/Vladimir Wrangel; 19bc British Museum (EA 63800); 19br Shutterstock/Jose Antonio Sanchez; 20tl Shutterstock/ Mirek
Hejnicki; 21tr Getty/Business Wire; 21cr Corbis/Hulton; 21br AKG/James Morris; 22tr Corbis/Stephen Vidler; 22c Art Archive/Dagli Orti; 22cr British Museum (EA 9565 &others); 24br Art Archive/Eygptian
Museum/Kharbine-Tapabor/Boistesselin; 25bc British Museum (EA 41548); 25br Art Archive/Musee du Louvre/Dagli Orti; 26l Art Archive/Staatliche Glypothek, Munich/Dagli Orti; 26br British Museum (EA
1694); 27 Shutterstock/Vitoriano Junior; 27cr Art Archive/Egyptian Museum, Turin/Dagli Orti; 27br Art Archive/ Jan Vinchon Numismatist, Paris/Dagli Orti; 28tl Shutterstock/Jose Ignacio Soto;
28tr Shutterstock/Baloncici; 28cl Shutterstock/Ragnarok; 28c British Museum; 28cr Shutterstock/BOSKO; 28bl Shutterstock/Adrian Lindley; 29 Shutterstock/stefanel; 30tl Shutterstock/Anastasios71;
30br Shutterstock/Paul Cowan; 31b Shutterstock/markrhiggins; 32c Shutterstock/James M House; 32–33 Shutterstock/Maximmal; 33tl AKG/Erich Lessing; 33cr AA/Agora Museum, Athens/Gianni Dagli Orti;
33cl With the kind permission of the Trustees of the British Museum; 33br Getty/Time & Life Pictures; 33r Shutterstock/Alice; 34tl AKG/Archives CDA/Guillo; 34bl iStockphoto; 35bc AKG/Erich Lessing;
37tl Corbis/Gianni Dagli Orti; 39bl AKG/SMPK Antiquities Museum; 40bl AKG/Musée du Louvre; 42tl Shutterstock/Panos Karapanagiotis; 42rc Shutterstock/RoxyFer; 42bl AKG/Erich Lessing; 42bc AA/
Musée du Louvre; 42br AA/Musée du Louvre; 43tl Shutterstock/Oleg Seleznev; 43r Shutterstock/bumihills; 43bl Bridgeman Art Library/Ancient Art & Architecture; 44tl AA/Superstock; 44bc AA/
Kanellopoulos Museum, Athens/Dagli Orti; 44r AKG/Kunsthistorisches Museum, Vienna; 45l Shutterstock/Denis Kornilov; 45tr With the kind permission of the Trustees of the British Museum; 45cc AA/
Agora Museum, Athens/Dagli Orti; 45cr AA/Soprintendenza Archaeologica, Salerno/Dagli Orti; 46–47 AA/ Musée Archéologique, Naples/Alfredo Dagli Orti; 46br Kobal/Warner Bros/Jaap Buitendijk;
47tr AKG/Bildarchiv Steffens; 48tr AA/Kanellopoulos Museum, Athens/Dagli Orti; 48cl AA/Museo Nazionale Terme, Rome/Gianni Dagli Orti; 49tr AA/Museo di Villa Giulia, Rome/Gianni Dagli Orti;
49cr Shutterstock/Evangelos; 50tl Marie-Lan Nguy; 50b Photolibrary/Waterframe; 51tl AKG/Nimatallah; 51cr Shutterstock/AISA-Everett; 51br PA/AP; 52cl Shutterstock/Brigida Soriano; 52cr Kobal/Warner
Bros/Jaap Buitendijk; 52bl Shutterstock/Jozef Sedmak; 52tr AA/Museo Nazionale Reggio, Calabria/Dagli Orti; 53 Shutterstock/Andrey Starostin; 54 Alamy/Gari Wyn Williams; 55 Frank Lane Picture
Agency/Sarah Rowland/Holt; 56–57 Corbis/Rudy Sulgan; 56cr Alamy/David Forster; 56c Corbis/Ed Kashi; 56bc AA/Archaeology Museum, Naples/Dagli Orti; 56br AA/Museo Civico Udine/Dagli Orti;
57tl Corbis/William Manning; 57c Alamy/Gavin Heller; 57bl Corbis/Wolfgang Meier/zefa; 57br (both) AA/Dagli Orti; 59tr AA/National Museum Bucharest/Dagli Orti; 61tl Getty Images/AFP; 61br British
Museum; 62br Shutterstock; 63tr Alamy/Marco Scataglini; 64–65 AA/Museo della Civita Romana/Dagli Orti; 64bl Shutterstock; 65tc Alamy/Mark Boulton; 65r Shutterstock; 65br Rex Features;
66tr Shutterstock/Oleg Mit; 66cl British Museum; 68ctr AA/Dagli Orti; 68c AA/Dagli Orti; 68bl Bridgeman Art Library (BAL)/Fitzwilliam Museum University of Cambridge; 68cbl AA/Musee du Louvre/Dagli
Orti; 68cbr BAL/ Musee du Louvre; 68br Alamy/London Art Archive; 70bl AA/Museo Capitolino/Dagli Orti; 71bl Corbis/Tobias Schwarz/Reuters; 72–73 background Shutterstock; 72tl AA/Museo
Capitolino/Dagli Orti; 72cl AA/Archaeological Museum, Naples/Dagli Orti; 72r AA/Archaeological Museum, Naples/Dagli Orti; 72c Alamy/London Art Archive; 72bc AA/Archaeology Museum, Naples/
Dagli Orti; 73tr The Ronald Grant Archive/HD Vision Studios/BBC/HBO; 73cl AA/Archaeology Museum, Naples/Dagli Orti; 73b BAL/Museum of London; 74–75 background Shutterstock; 74bl AA/Navy
Historical Service, Vincennes/Dagli Orti; 74r AA/British Library; 75cl Corbis/Vincent Kessler/Reuters; 75c Corbis/George D. Lepp; 75cl AA/Musee du Chateau de Versailles/Dagli Orti; 75bl Corbis/Bob Krist;
75br PA/AP/Marianna Bertagnolli; 76l Shutterstock/Vera Bogaerts; 76cl Art Archive/Villa of the Mysteries Pompeii/Dagli Orti; 76bl Shutterstock/Pavle Marjanovic; 76tr Photolibrary/Davis McCardle;
76br The Little Entertainment Group.

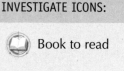

INVESTIGATE ICONS:

Book to read

Place to visit

Website to visit

CONTENTS

ANCIENT EGYPT

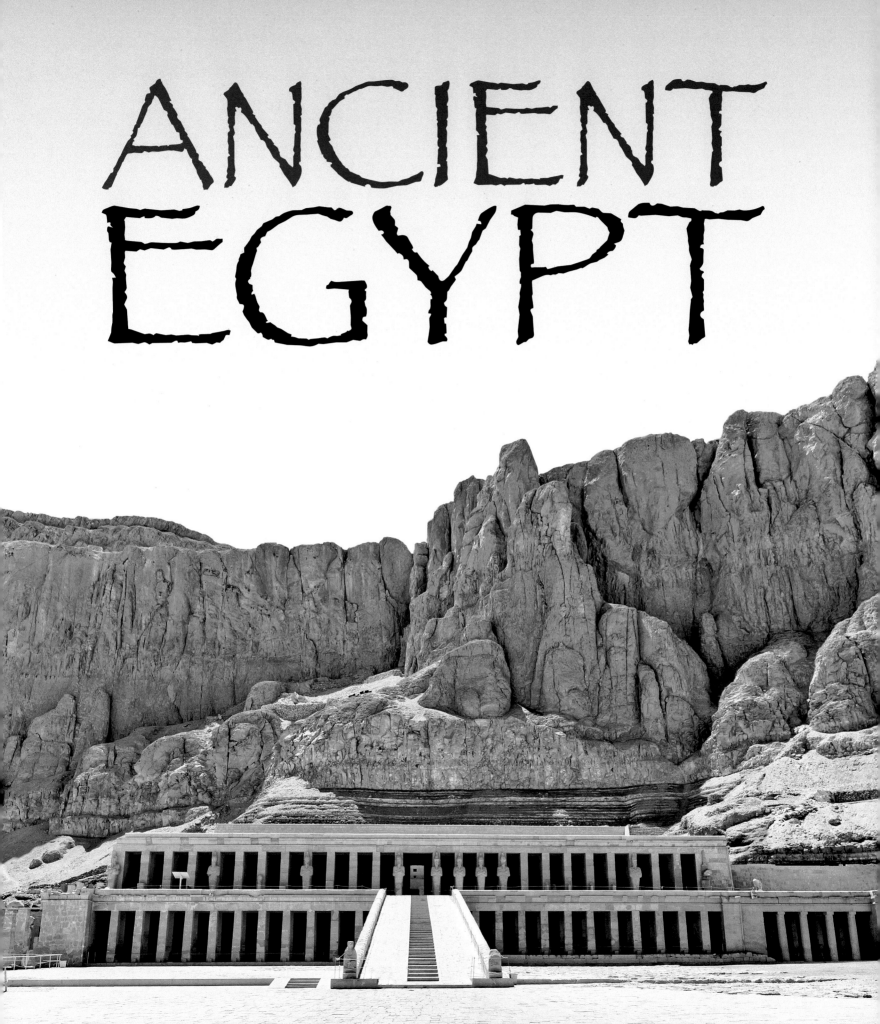

The black border shows the boundaries of modern-day Egypt. The highlighted section is the area of ancient Egypt shown on these two pages.

RIVER OF LIFE

The River Nile brought life to the desert lands of Egypt. On its banks, the ancient Egyptians built an extraordinary civilization that lasted for more than 3,000 years. They used the river to transport goods and armies, raised crops on its floodplains and built great cities on its banks.

"The Nile, forever new and old,
Among the living and the dead,
Its mighty, mystic stream has rolled."

Henry Wadsworth Longfellow
from The Golden Legend

Mediterranean Sea

Red Sea∞

Gulf of Suez

LOWER EGYPT

NILE DELTA

In the north, the river separates into different branches, creating the triangular marshlands of the delta.

Egypt's most famous pyramids were built on the Giza Plateau, just south of the delta.

• ALEXANDRIA

GIZA •
• SAQQARA
• MEMPHIS

The Step Pyramid at Saqqara was the first pyramid built in Egypt.

FAIYUM OASIS

RIVER NILE

• AKHETATEN (AMARNA)

ABYDOS •

Voyage in time

A journey down the River Nile is a journey through history. The rulers of Egypt were known as the Lords of the Two Lands. Upper Egypt was the Nile valley in the south. Lower Egypt was the north, mainly the area of the delta. Capital cities moved to various places on the Nile as the leaders of different families became pharaohs.

Black and red

The ancient Egyptians called the fertile strip near the River Nile *Kemet*, which means 'the black land'. They associated the colour black with life rather than death because it was the colour of their soil. Their word for the harsh, desert regions that covered most of Egypt was *Deshret*, which means 'the red land'.

> INUNDATION – *the annual flooding of the River Nile during the summer*

● THE INUNDATION

Every year, the River Nile flooded, depositing a rich layer of black silt either side of the banks. This was called the inundation. The crops grown in the enriched soil included barley, emmer wheat, lentils, figs, flax, grapes, pomegranates and cucumbers. The shaduf (right) that the Egyptians invented to lift water from the river for irrigation is still used today.

The temple of Amun was built near the great trading city of Thebes, on the east bank of the river.

EASTERN DESERT

VALLEY OF THE KINGS

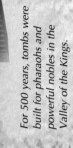

For 500 years, tombs were built for pharaohs and powerful nobles in the Valley of the Kings.

● KARNAK
● LUXOR

VALLEY OF THE QUEENS (THEBES)

RIVER NILE

EDFU ●

● ASWAN
● PHILAE

WESTERN DESERT

UPPER EGYPT

Valley transport

Wooden sailing boats have sailed down the protected waters of the Nile for more than 5,000 years. The river is the longest in the world, but through the narrow Nile valley it is never more than 19km across.

Ramesses II's temples at Abu Simbel marked the southern part of the Egyptian empire, where the land bordered Nubia (today's Sudan).

● ABU SIMBEL

God of the flood

Hapy was the god of the annual inundation. The Egyptians made offerings to him to make sure that there would be just the right level of flooding for their crops. He was said to be the husband of both the vulture-goddess Nekhbet, protector of Upper Egypt, and the cobra-goddess Wadjyt, protector of Lower Egypt.

⟩ Even today, 90 per cent of Egypt is desert and more than 95 per cent of the population live in the Nile valley.

HIERARCHY - government by a system of people ranked one above another

PHARAOH GOD

Ramesses II was worshipped as a living god. He ordered two temples to be carved in sandstone cliffs at Abu Simbel in Nubia. This one has giant carvings of the gods, including Ramesses himself.

As ruler of the nation, the pharaoh represented the gods – about 1,500 of them. Both the pharaoh and the ordinary people worshipped these gods and gave them gifts. This ensured that the annual flood took place and order was upheld. When the pharaoh died, he became protector of the dead and helped their rebirth into a new life.

Gifts to the gods

Discovered in a tomb near Medinet Habu, the extraordinary Great Harris Papyrus, written during the reign of Ramesses IV, celebrates Ramesses III. It shows the pharaoh making offerings to different groups of gods, including the ones shown below. The three gods on the left are the triad of Memphis, and the next three the triad of Thebes.

Ptah was a creator god and the god of craftsmen.

Sekhmet was Ptah's wife and the goddess of war.

Nefertem was Ptah and Sekhmet's son, and was god of the lotus flower.

Khons was the moon god, and son of Amun and Mut.

> The word 'pharaoh' means 'the Great House' and symbolized the royal palaces in which the pharaoh lived.

Life and death

On Earth, the sun-god in his various guises over the centuries as Ra, Ra-Harakhty, Amun and Amun-Ra was the dominant deity. In the afterlife, the lord of the dead, Osiris, and the god of mummification, the jackal-headed Anubis (left), ruled supreme.

⊖ RULING THE KINGDOM

The pharaoh had absolute power over his subjects. However, in practice he had to rule through a hierarchy of officials. The chief adviser was the vizier, or first minister, followed by other high officials, diplomats and the priests, who helped govern the different parts of Egypt. Scribes were in charge of keeping all records and issuing rules of law.

sculpture of an Egyptian scribe

www.ancientegypt.co.uk/gods/explore/main.html

Mut was Amun's wife, daughter of the sun-god Ra and the mother goddess.

The roles of gods changed over time and many gods took multiple forms.

Amun was the king of gods and a creator god.

Ramesses III gave 309,950 sacks of grain, metals and semi-precious gems to the Theban triad alone.

PALACE LIFE

A pharaoh owned several palaces, and moved with his household from one to the other by royal barge on the River Nile. He also had several wives, one of whom was his chief wife and queen. Egyptian nobles who were in favour would be invited to send their children to court where they could live and study alongside the royal children.

A royal banquet

Egyptians enjoyed entertaining, and feasts at the palace were elaborate affairs. The pharaoh, his chief wife and honoured guests watched from a raised dais. The remaining guests were seated at tables around the room. They wore garlands and offered flowers to each other as they ate. Servants carried in roast game, fish, vegetables and fruit, while musicians, dancers and acrobats entertained them.

MENAGERIE – a collection of wild or exotic animals, kept for exhibition

Women's tunics could cover one or both shoulders, or were worn with shoulder straps.

Men usually wore linen kilts, wrapped around the waist.

 > The toilet in an Egyptian palace was a low, wooden stool with a hole cut in the seat.

Hieroglyphs were used to decorate the palace pillars.

Artistic licence

This picture shows women at a feast. In their hands are bunches of lotus flowers, the symbol of rebirth and renewal. On their heads are 'perfume cones'. These cones are thought to be a device used by the artist to indicate that the women are wearing perfume.

Singers and musicians entertained the palace guests.

Exotic animals

Some pharaohs kept menageries. Many of the animals were given to them by foreign kings, but others were collected when the pharaoh waged war. Ramesses II had a pet lion that accompanied him into battle. Thutmose III kept antelopes, leopards, ostriches, elephants, rhinoceroses and chickens in his botanical gardens (left).

⊖ JEWELLERY AND MAKE-UP

Wealthy Egyptians took great care with their appearance for feasts. Both men and women painted heavy black lines in kohl around the eyes, and women rubbed rouge into their cheeks. Anklets and rings were worn for their beauty and as a protection from evil.

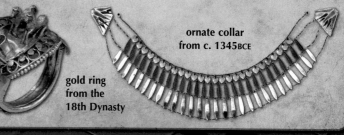

ornate collar from c. 1345BCE

gold ring from the 18th Dynasty

SCRIBE STORY

A scribe's profession was a respected one in ancient Egypt. The Egyptians valued learning, and all the offices of state were open to a scribe because he could read and write in hieroglyphs (picture symbols). Nebamun was 'the Scribe and Grain accountant in the Granary of Amun' in Thebes, who died in about 1350BCE. Paintings from his tomb-chapel at Dra Abu el-Naga, opposite Thebes, give us an insight into his life.

Tomb hunter

Paintings on the walls of tombs were laden with symbolism. This wall-painting is symbolic in its intention to help Nebamun's rebirth in the afterlife. The Egyptians believed that the world was born out of the marshy waters of chaos. Nebamun's hunting symbolizes his triumph over the chaos in nature, while various symbols of the sun-god ensure Nebamun's rebirth, just like the sun reappearing in the sky every day.

The Painter

These six cups were found by the side of a mummy nicknamed 'The Painter' during an excavation at Hawara. They are made of clay from the River Nile. The paintbrush is made from fine palm fibres cut at one end, and there are traces of red pigment on the end of the brush.

 ❯ The ancient Egyptians believed that carving a name could help a person live forever.

www.britishmuseum.org/explore/galleries/ancient_egypt/room_61_tomb-chapel_nebamun.aspx

KEY

1 Nebamun stands on a small papyrus boat. In his left hand is a snake-headed throwing stick, which is being used to hunt waterfowl.

2 Hatshepsut, Nebamun's wife, is dressed in her finest clothes and crowned with lotus flowers and a perfume cone. She is ready for her journey into the afterlife.

3 Nebamun's daughter sits between his legs, picking lotus flowers. Her youth is shown by the lack of clothes and the sidelock (single braid of hair).

4 A tawny cat attacks several birds. The gold leaf on the cat's eye suggests that it represents the sun-god Ra who was reborn every day at dawn.

5 Nebamun's white kilt and overkilt are made of fine linen to represent his wealth. His stomach has small rolls of fat to further indicate his prosperity.

6 A red goose, an animal sacred to Amun, sits on the prow of the boat.

7 On the top of a thick clump of papyrus reeds – marsh plants that were used to make the paper for scribes – are three nests containing bird eggs.

8 The poisonous puffer fish is still found in the River Nile today.

Hieroglyphs

Egyptians composed names for everything in their world using picture symbols called hieroglyphs. Here, Rehotep, a prince of the 4th Dynasty, is seated in front of a table on which there are offerings to sustain him in the afterlife. These gifts, including incense, eye-paint, wine and dates, are described in the hieroglyphs.

'Egyptian blue' pigment is a man-made copper calcium silicate.

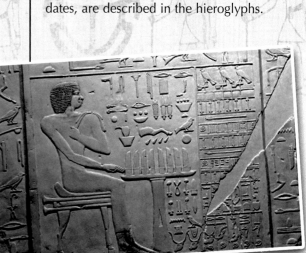

LIFE AT HOME

Egyptian houses were built of bricks made of mud and straw, and dried in the sun. In the towns, some of the finer houses were two storeys high and had bathrooms and toilets. Their walls were plastered and painted with geometric patterns and scenes of plants and birds. During hot weather, many people slept on the roof and sometimes cooked there as well. Household waste was buried in pits, or thrown in the river or into the street. Water was drawn from public or private wells.

servants' quarters

servants tending garden

ma
entra

⊜ HOME FURNISHINGS

Wealthy homes had tiled floors and painted walls. Furniture was minimal and included low stools, chests, tables and beds. Poor people slept on a straw mat, with headrests that had protective images to ward off scorpions and bad dreams.

stone gaming board with pottery playing pieces

wooden toy cat with moveable mouth

Egyptians had large families, and the children stayed at home until their early teens. Many toys and games have been found in excavations, and they often had birds or dogs as pets. The boys went to school, but the girls helped in the home.

"I am the most beautiful tree in the garden
And for all times, I shall remain.
The beloved and her brother
Stroll under my branches,
Intoxicated from wines and spirits,
Steeped in oil and fragrant essences."

Turin Papyrus
19th Dynasty

Garden houses

In the countryside, the houses of wealthy Egyptians were set in large, formal gardens surrounded by high walls. At this nobleman's garden-house at Akhetaten, trees were grown both for shade and their fruit, which included dates, figs, pomegranates and nuts. Vines were planted in straight rows between ponds stocked with fish.

> Baboons were trained to climb fig trees and pick the ripe fruit for their owners.

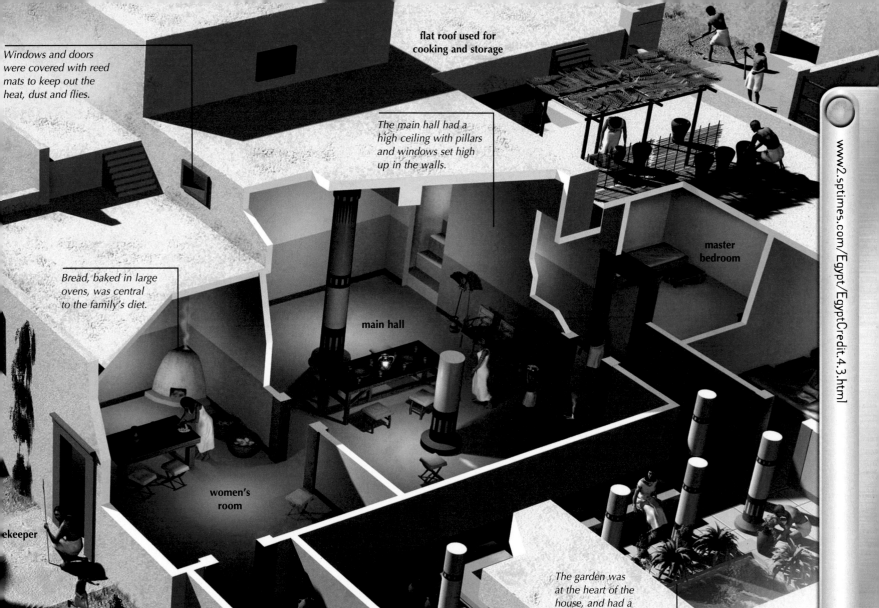

Windows and doors were covered with reed mats to keep out the heat, dust and flies.

flat roof used for cooking and storage

The main hall had a high ceiling with pillars and windows set high up in the walls.

master bedroom

Bread, baked in large ovens, was central to the family's diet.

main hall

women's room

ekeeper

The garden was at the heart of the house, and had a pool with exotic fish.

garden

In the towns

There were set areas used for particular purposes in all the houses in ancient Egypt, from a basic, mudbrick house to a wealthy home in town (above). The father of the family received guests in a reception area, the mother and children had a private domain, and there was an area for routine tasks, such as food preparation and other everyday chores.

Household gods

There were niches (small hollows) in the house walls where the statues of protective household gods and goddesses were kept. Bes (right), the bearded dwarf-god, frightened away evil spirits, while Bastet, the cat-goddess, warded off infectious diseases. Tawaret, with the head of a hippopotamus, protected women during pregnancy and childbirth.

PYRAMID BUILDER

It took about 20 years and the labour of thousands of men to build one of the Seven Wonders of the Ancient World, the Great Pyramid of Khufu at Giza. Around 5,000 of the workers were full-time employees of the pharaoh, while 20,000 were farm workers, conscripted for a few months of each year when the River Nile flooded the fields.

Workers' graffiti

The workers were organized into crews by their supervisors, to develop a competitive team spirit. A crew would be of about 2,000 men, split into large gangs that were then subdivided and given specific tasks. Graffiti shows that the crews at Giza gave themselves names such as 'Friends of Khufu' and 'Drunkards of Menkaure'.

bakers

fishmongers

physician

Village of the workers

Purpose-built villages supported the daily lives of the pyramid workers. The villages were fully functioning, with streets, houses, shops and a cemetery. The workers and their families were cared for by a dentist and physician. This is known because archaeologists have found remains of pyramid workers at Giza that show that the Egyptians knew how to realign broken bones.

> Farm labourers had daily rations of ten loaves and a measure of beer.

a Giza team name: 'The White Crown of Khufu is Powerful'

The Great Pyramid is made of some 2.3 million blocks of stone, weighing 2.25 to 13.5 tonnes each.

Up to 30,000 workers built the three pyramids at Giza over a period of 80 years.

butchers

granary

blacksmith

copper works

MASTER BUILDERS

The pyramid builders dragged the large blocks of stone for the Great Pyramid 300m across the desert from the quarry and up ramps to each level as the pyramid grew. They fitted them into place with tools that were not unlike those in use today. Special blocks of white limestone, trimmed to make a smooth surface, covered the outside of the pyramid, and the top was covered in metal to glint in the sunlight.

saw

chisel

mallet

STAIRWAYS TO HEAVEN

The pyramid complex at Giza is on a plateau just south of the modern city of Cairo.

The Egyptians believed that when a pharaoh died, the sun-god Ra strengthened the rays of the sun to allow the ruler to climb to the sky. The shape of a pyramid provided the 'stairway to heaven' that was needed. The earliest pyramids were designed in steps. Later, architects competed with one another to build the perfect pyramid.

Menkaure (reigned c. 2532–2504BCE) built the third and smallest pyramid, which was 65.5m tall.

"All the world fears time, but time fears the pyramids."

Arab proverb

Pyramids of Giza

During the 4th Dynasty, three pharaohs contributed to what is the most famous pyramid complex of all. Located at Giza, the largest structure, the Great Pyramid, is the only one of the Seven Wonders of the Ancient World still standing. Near the smallest structure, the pyramid of Menkaure, stand three small pyramids that were built for queens.

> The Great Pyramid was the tallest man-made structure in the world for more than 3,800 years.

www.pbs.org/wgbh/nova/pyramid/explore/5

Step Pyramid

The first pyramid to be built in Egypt was for the 3rd Dynasty pharaoh King Djoser. Constructed at Saqqara in c. 2650–2575BCE, it began as a normal mastaba, or tomb, which was a single-storey rectangular building with underground rooms for the burial chambers. Later, more mastabas were added on top, until it reached a height of 60m.

The Step Pyramid of Djoser rises in six stages.

Khufu (reigned c. 2589–2566BCE), built the Great Pyramid, which was 146.5m tall.

Khafre (reigned c. 2558–2532BCE) built the second largest pyramid at Giza, which was 143.5m tall.

Architect to the pharaoh

Imhotep was Djoser's vizier and architect, and is credited with being the builder of the Step Pyramid. The Egyptian historian Manetho claims that the architect invented the technique of building in dressed stone. He also writes about Imhotep's list of 'instructions' and works on medicine, but nothing has survived of these.

Bent Pyramid

In the first attempt at building a true pyramid with smooth sides, architects began a project at the necropolis of Dahshur, but it was at too steep an angle. Cracks began to appear, so they changed the angle to make the slope more gradual. This resulted in what is now known as the Bent Pyramid of Sneferu, a pharaoh of the 4th Dynasty.

The Bent Pyramid of Sneferu stood 105m tall.

VALLEY OF THE KINGS

In the 18th Dynasty, the pharaohs abandoned pyramid building because these structures were out in the open and difficult to defend against tomb raiders. Instead, they began to build rock-cut tombs in the hills near the west bank of the River Nile, opposite Thebes. The Valley of the Kings, surrounded by easily defended cliffs, remained in use until the end of the 20th Dynasty. At least 63 tombs have been excavated there.

Find of the century

On 4 November 1922, a team led by English Egyptologist Howard Carter uncovered the first of 16 descending steps into the Valley of the Kings. They had discovered the entrance to the tomb of the boy pharaoh Tutankhamun (reigned 1336–1327 BCE), containing many of the possessions originally placed in there for the pharaoh to use in the afterlife.

The red sandstone sarcophagus of Tutankhamun contained three coffins nesting inside one another.

Ransacked by robbers, the annex contained empty containers and artefacts.

annex

antechamber

> SHRINE - *a container for the statue of a god or the remains of a dead person*

treasury

One of the four miniature gold coffins, decorated with coloured glass and semi-precious stones, that contained viscera (internal body organs).

Boats, gilded figures and a superb canopic chest were among the treasures found here.

Historic discovery

Howard Carter (kneeling) peers at Tutankhamun's sarcophagus through the open doors of the four gilded shrines nesting inside one another in the burial chamber. The tomb had been broken into by tomb raiders on at least two occasions, but resealed by the necropolis guards.

passage

staircase

● PAINTED LEGACY

One of the largest tombs in the Valley of the Kings is that of Seti I (reigned 1294–1279 BCE). It is more than 120m long, and dug deep into a hillside. Discovered in 1817 by an Italian explorer, Giovanni Battista Belzoni, it has remarkable wall-paintings. The ceiling in the crypt is vaulted and painted with stars.

the astronomical ceiling in the crypt

This room's contents included dismantled chariots, food, animal-shaped beds, thrones, jewellery and sandals.

❯ The fingerprints of one of the men who robbed Tutankhamun's tomb are still visible inside a jar of ointment.

www.tutankhamun-exhibition.co.uk/

MUMMIFICATION

When an ancient Egyptian died, it was essential that the body was preserved as a resting-place for the spirit. The deceased was taken to the *per nefer*, or 'perfect house', where embalmers carried out a mummification process that took up to 70 days. This was intended to ensure the survival of the dead person for all eternity. Statues were also commissioned, which could stand in for the body if it was somehow destroyed.

Animals, such as cats, monkeys and crocodiles, were mummified for their preservation as pets, sacred animals or gifts for the gods.

⊖ OPENING OF THE MOUTH

When the mummy was ready to be placed in the coffin, a ritual called the 'Opening of the Mouth' was performed by the dead person's son or heir wearing the mask of Anubis, god of mummification. The ceremony was vital because it meant that the dead person could eat, drink and move around in the afterlife.

Ay, Tutankhamun's successor, stands before Osiris holding the ceremonial *setep*, or *adze*.

Canopic jars

The liver, intestines, stomach and lungs were removed during mummification. They were stored for protection in four special containers called canopic jars. The heart was left inside the body so that it could be weighed in the afterlife. The stoppers of these jars represent the four sons of Horus, the canopic deities.

In the *ibu*, the place of purification, the embalmers first wash the body with palm wine and then rinse it with water taken from the River Nile.

Here, the stomach is being removed, before being washed, packed with natron and placed in the canopic jar representing the jackal-headed god Duamutef.

The embalmers use a long hook to smash the brain, and pull it out through the nostrils. Then the whole body is stuffed with and covered in natron.

After 40 days, the body is washed out with Nile water, oiled and perfumed. The brain cavity is filled with resin or linen and artificial eyes are added.

 > A scarab beetle amulet was placed over the heart to ensure it was not separated from the body.

Preparing the dead

The process of mummification changed over time. To begin with, it was available only to kings, but by the New Kingdom (c. 1550–1070BCE) it was the practice for anyone that could afford it. The *hery seshta*, or master of secrets, was in charge and took the role of the jackal-god Anubis. Natron salt crystals were used to dehydrate, or dry out, the body. A priest was on hand to recite spells and prayers.

The master of secrets inserts protective amulets between the wrappings while bandaging the body.

The body is stuffed with dry material, such as sawdust and leaves (above), then oiled again. Finally, it is wrapped in many layers of linen (right) in a process that takes up to 15 days.

www.ancientegypt.co.uk/mummies/story/main.html

THE FINAL JOURNEY

The coffin was carried inside the tomb, together with goods for the deceased to use in the afterlife. Egyptians believed that during their journey through the underworld, they had to win their place in the afterlife. They were judged on their behaviour during their lifetime at a ceremony called the 'Weighing of the Heart'.

The underworld

The Egyptians believed that the path to the underworld was full of dangers, such as snakes and crocodiles. Armed with spells, some written on coffins and others on scrolls of papyrus called 'Books of the Dead', the deceased would be able to overcome all the dangers and reach the afterlife.

"May I walk every day on the banks of the water, may my soul rest on the branches of the trees which I planted, may I refresh myself under the shadow of my sycamore."

Egyptian tomb description

c. 1400BCE

Ancestor gods

When a pharaoh died, many personal items were placed with them in the coffin. Ahhotep I was a powerful queen during the 17th Dynasty. This is her funerary bracelet, made of gold and lapis lazuli. It shows the ancestor souls of the cities of Pe and Nekhen. They are lifting their hands in jubilation to wish the pharaoh 'all life and sovereignty'.

> Ancient Egyptians provided for the afterlife in a way that reflected their lifestyles on Earth.

the goddess Ammut

Anubis, god
of the dead

Heavy heart

Jackal-headed god Anubis weighed the heart of the deceased
against the feather of Maat, goddess of truth and justice. If the
heart was too heavy, it would be eaten by crocodile-headed
Ammut, the eater of the dead. The deceased would then die
a second death and cease to exist.

Painted coffins

Coffins depicted the person as they would like to look for eternity.
They were covered in spells to protect the deceased and preserve
their spirit. Early coffins were made of wood and were usually
rectangular. Later, body-shaped inner coffins (right) made of
wood or metal were placed inside outer coffins (far right).

● FUNERARY GOODS

Male and female shabti (figures
made in the image of servants) were
buried with the dead. They were
inscribed with a special formula
that enabled the servants to carry
out manual work on behalf of the
dead person. They were normally
made of faience or wood.

**painted wooden shabti figures of
the Theban priestess Henutmehyt**

END OF A CIVILIZATION

ASP - a family of snakes that includes the very poisonous Egyptian cobra and the horned viper of North Africa

From the 7th century BCE, Egypt was invaded by foreign powers. These included the Assyrians, the Persians, and the Macedonian Greeks led by Alexander the Great. In 309BCE, Alexander's general, Ptolemy, founded a Greek-speaking dynasty that ruled from Alexandria. Egypt retained its identity until the death of the last Greek ruler, Cleopatra, in 30BCE, when Egypt became part of the Roman empire.

Alexander the Great

In 332BCE, the 24-year-old Alexander III of Macedon marched into Egypt. He was welcomed as a liberator because the Egyptians had suffered exploitation and taxes during the occupation by the Persians, who also did not respect their traditions. Alexander was anointed pharaoh at Memphis on 14 November, but he left Egypt only six months after he arrived.

Apis bull

Alexander was acutely aware of the need to show respect for Egyptian customs. In Upper Egypt, he found it easy to think of Amun as a form of the chief Greek god, Zeus. In Lower Egypt, he offered sacrifices to the Apis bull, the cult animal of the creator god Ptah.

 Cleopatra spoke several languages and was the only Ptolemaic pharaoh who learned Egyptian.

Alexandria

During his stay in Egypt, Alexander founded the city of Alexandria on the Mediterranean coast, but did not live to see it completed. The city later became the capital of Egypt under the Ptolemaic kings. It was famous for its lighthouse at Pharos (right) and its library, which was the largest in the ancient world.

Cultural identity

This is the mummy case of Artemidorus, who died in about 100–120CE in Hawara, Egypt. It is a good example of the merging of different cultures. The portrait is in the Roman style, his Greek personal name is inscribed on it, and the mummy has been preserved in the traditional Egyptian way.

● FINAL PHARAOH

Cleopatra VII Philopator (reigned 51–30BCE) originally shared power with her brothers, Ptolemy XIII and Ptolemy XIV. She became sole ruler with the support of Julius Caesar, and then Caesar's general, Mark Antony. She committed suicide after losing to the Romans at the Battle of Actium.

Cleopatra killed herself with the bite of an asp.

Alexander's general reigned as Ptolemy (305–282BCE). He consolidated Greek rule in Egypt and founded the legendary library of Alexandria.

INVESTIGATE

Discover how archaeologists and other experts have unearthed the history of the extraordinary civilization of ancient Egypt by checking out museums, art galleries, books and websites.

ancient Egyptian hieroglyphs

scarab beetle, the ancient Egyptian symbol for rebirth

Museums and art galleries

Visit the many museums, art galleries and special exhibitions displaying objects that archaeologists have discovered, and depictions of life in ancient Egypt.

📖 *The Usborne Encyclopedia of Ancient Egypt* by Gill Harvey and Struan Reid (Usborne)

◆ British Museum, Great Russell Street, London WC1V 3DG, UK

🔘 www.metmuseum.org/collections/galleries

elaborately patterned glass jar of the 18th Dynasty

Books and magazines

Find out facts for yourself by reading information books and specialist magazines about ancient Egypt.

📖 *Lifelines: Cleopatra* by Adèle Geras (Kingfisher)

◆ Visit your local library to discover a whole range of books about ancient Egypt.

🔘 http://ngm.nationalgeographic.com/ngm/egypt/egyptfile.html

Great Sphinx at Giza, built by Khafre

people have sailed down the Nile for thousands of years

Television and the movies

Follow documentaries and dramas about the personalities that ruled ancient Egypt and watch films that portray life along the banks of the Nile.

📀 *Unlocking the Great Pyramid* by Bob Brier (National Geographic DVD)

◆ The History Channel: Ancient Egypt

🔘 www.ancientnile.co.uk/films.php

ANCIENT
GREECE

CIVILIZATION – a society that has developed government, laws, arts, science and technology

ILLYRIA

MACEDONIA

gold coin of Philip II of Macedon showing the hero Heracles

THRACE

About 80 per cent of the Greek mainland is taken up by mountains and hills.

CHALCIDICE

AEGEAN SEA

EPIRUS

Mount Olympus, home of the gods

MOUNT OLYMPUS

CORFU

PINDUS MOUNTAINS

THESSALY

GREECE CYNOSCEPHALAE •

AETOLIA

THERMOPYLAE •

LOCRIS   DELPHI •

PHOCIS

• ORCHOMENUS

EUBOEA

• CHALCIS

• ERETRIA

BOEOTIA

• THEBES

ACHAEA

Delphi, a major religious site

• PLATAEA

ATTICA   • MARATHON

MEGARA •   SALAMIS •

• ATHENS

• ELIS

CORINTH •

NEMEA •

PIRAEUS •

OLYMPIA

MYCENAE •

ARGOS •   • TIRYNS

• EPIDAURUS

Parthenon, a temple that overlooks the city of Athens, the most powerful state in Greece, c. 400s BCE

ANCIENT CIVILIZATIONS

Ruined cities, temples and theatres can still be seen in Greece. Most date from the great age of the Greek city-states, between the 700s and 300s BCE. The civilizations that flourished in Greece between 5,000 and 2,300 years ago still affect the way we see the world today.

PELOPONNESE

MESSENIA

• SPARTA

LACONIA

• PYLOS

statue of Zeus at Olympia, c. 432BCE

Sparta, a military state

IONIAN SEA

VOYAGE TO GREECE

Greece can be visited by ship, crossing the dark-blue waters of the Aegean or Ionian seas. Island after island appears on the horizon. Beyond them lies the Greek mainland, where mountains and rocky shores surround plains and groves of olive trees. The climate is hot and dry in summer, but mild and moist in winter. In ancient times this beautiful, sunny land was called Hellas.

ACROSS THE WAVES

These fish and dolphins were painted at the palace of Knossos on the island of Crete more than 3,500 years ago. Greece is a land of coasts and islands. Its seas were sailed by fishermen, merchants, pirates and warriors.

MEDITERRANEAN SEA

> Earthquakes are common in Greece. They were said to be the work of the god Poseidon.

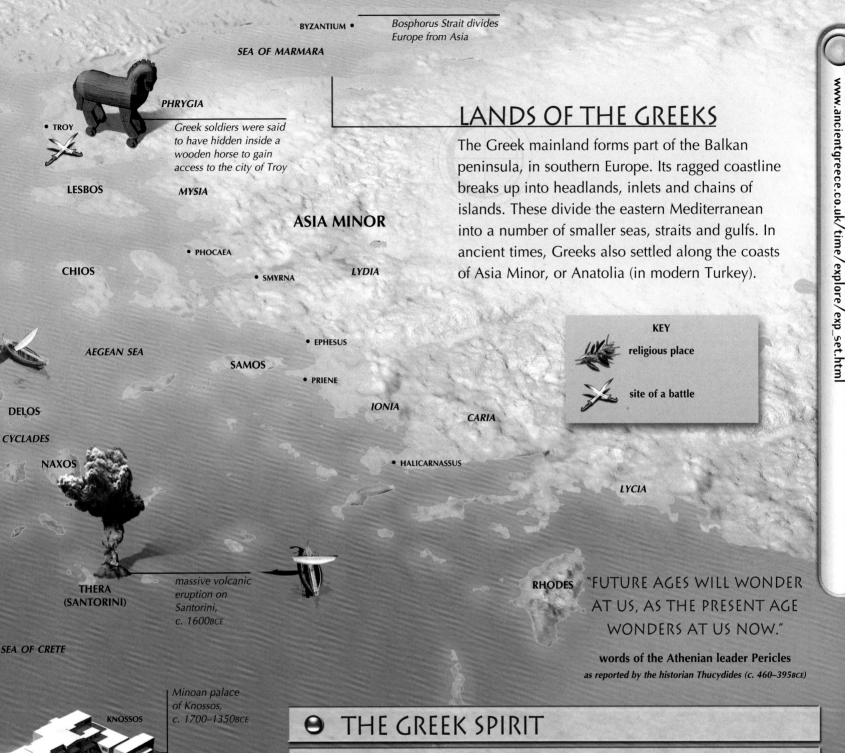

BLACK SEA

BYZANTIUM •

Bosphorus Strait divides
Europe from Asia

SEA OF MARMARA

PHRYGIA

• TROY

Greek soldiers were said
to have hidden inside a
wooden horse to gain
access to the city of Troy

LESBOS   MYSIA

ASIA MINOR

• PHOCAEA

CHIOS   • SMYRNA   LYDIA

LANDS OF THE GREEKS

The Greek mainland forms part of the Balkan peninsula, in southern Europe. Its ragged coastline breaks up into headlands, inlets and chains of islands. These divide the eastern Mediterranean into a number of smaller seas, straits and gulfs. In ancient times, Greeks also settled along the coasts of Asia Minor, or Anatolia (in modern Turkey).

• EPHESUS

AEGEAN SEA   SAMOS

• PRIENE

DELOS   IONIA   CARIA

CYCLADES

NAXOS

• HALICARNASSUS

LYCIA

KEY

🌿 religious place

⚔ site of a battle

THERA
(SANTORINI)

massive volcanic
eruption on
Santorini,
c. 1600BCE

RHODES   "FUTURE AGES WILL WONDER AT US, AS THE PRESENT AGE WONDERS AT US NOW."

words of the Athenian leader Pericles
as reported by the historian Thucydides (c. 460–395BCE)

SEA OF CRETE

Minoan palace
of Knossos,
c. 1700–1350BCE

KNOSSOS

⊖ THE GREEK SPIRIT

For most of its history, Greece was not united as a single nation. Instead, it was made up of rival cities and small city-states. Sometimes these joined forces, but often they fought against each other. Even so, throughout most of their history, all Greeks shared similar ways of life, the same language, view of the world and religious practices.

CRETE

Greek horsemen ride through Athens

www.ancientgreece.co.uk/time/explore/exp_set.html

ATHENS IN ITS GLORY

During the 400s BCE, Athens experienced a golden age. Its large fleet of warships made it the most powerful of the Greek city-states. Athens benefited from the Attica region's rich silver mines and grew wealthy through trade. The city became an exciting centre of discussion and new ideas, of philosophy, politics, drama, writing, sculpture, architecture and fine craft skills.

THE GODDESS CITY

Athens was built around a high, rocky stronghold, or Acropolis. On top of this was the Parthenon, a great temple to the goddess Athena, who protected the city. It housed a statue of ivory and gold, almost 13m high. The city spread out below, a sea of tiled roofs and white walls. There were houses and courtyards, law courts and market halls. About 250,000 people may have lived in Athens and the surrounding region.

The Parthenon was a temple made from white marble. This rich stone displayed the wealth of the city.

> It was said that Athena created the olive tree as a gift for the city of Athens.

SILVER OWL

Athenians minted coins of silver. This one shows an owl, the emblem of Athena, the goddess of wisdom. Owl coins were traded for goods across the ancient world.

● PEOPLE POWER

Our word 'politics' comes from *polis*, Greek for 'city-state'. Athens was the first state to attempt to be ruled by its own people. This system was called *demokratía* or democracy. All citizens could attend the assembly to make political decisions. Court cases were decided by juries of hundreds of citizens. But women and slaves were excluded from democracy.

jurors' tickets used in the *dikasterion* (law court) in Athens, in the 4th century BCE

"OUR CONSTITUTION IS NAMED A DEMOCRACY, BECAUSE IT IS IN THE HANDS NOT OF THE FEW BUT OF THE MANY."

Thucydides (c. 460–400BCE)
Athenian politician and historian, from his
History of the Peloponnesian War, Book 1 *(431BCE)*

THE AGE OF PERICLES

Pericles lived from about 495 to 429BCE. He was a great Athenian statesman, a brilliant public speaker, and a military leader who also encouraged the arts and the creation of beautiful architecture.

RIVAL POWERS

After the war with Persia, the Greek city-states formed a military alliance, called the Delian League, controlled by Athens. Its power was challenged by a Peloponnesian League, led by Sparta. From 431 to 404BCE, Greek fought against Greek, by land and sea.

TO VICTORY

Warriors and chariots decorate the rim of this bronze krater, a vase used for mixing wine and water. It was made in Laconia around 530BCE, but found far away in France. Bronze work was a key export from Laconia.

design celebrating the victory of warriors

shield (hoplon) of bronze, wood and leather

stabbing spear, 2m to 3m long

helmet with horsehair crest

THE SNARLING FOX

A Spartan boy once stole a fox. He hid it beneath his cloak. When challenged, he refused to own up, even though the fox was gnawing and biting. He died of his wounds. The Spartans saw no shame in stealing, only in being found out.

FIGHTING FIT

In Sparta, the physically weak might be killed at birth. From an early age, Spartan boys were trained in physical exercise, wrestling and combat. Cowards ('tremblers') were despised.

learning to wrestle

> HOPLITE – *an armed foot soldier in ancient Greece*

bronze greave
(shin guard) to
protect lower leg

SHIELDS
OF SPARTA

Who needs stone walls around their city if they have the bravest warriors? That was the proud boast of the city-state of Sparta. The Spartans were certainly the toughest fighters in Greece. They conquered the regions of Laconia and Messenia in the south by about 550BCE and forced the local people to work for them as labourers called 'helots'. This left the Spartans free – to train for war.

THE RED CLOAKS

At the age of seven, Spartan boys were taken from their parents and sent to live in a barracks with others of the same age. The discipline was very harsh. From the age of 20, a male could wear the famous red cloak of a Spartan warrior, or hoplite (literally meaning 'shield-bearer'). The hoplite could be called up to fight at any time until he reached the age of 60. Their armour was expensive and each hoplite had to buy his own. Dead hoplites were carried from the battlefield on their shields.

SPARTAN GIRLS

Girls in Sparta were taught to race and wrestle. Most Greeks were shocked by this. Elsewhere, young women were expected to stay inside their house, spin and weave wool, and give birth to children.

❯ The Spartans were ruled not by one king, but by two at the same time.

SHIPS AT WAR

After 490BCE, the city-state of Athens built a large navy. Soon it ruled the waves. Hundreds of warships could dock at Piraeus, the city's seaport. The fastest type of ship was the trireme, which used oar power to ram and sink the enemy. It had a mast with a single, square sail, but in battle the deck was stripped bare for action.

Two long sweeps (steering oars) are operated by a helmsman at the stern.

TRIREME – *a warship with three banks of oars*

A double flute called an aulos is blown to help the oarsmen keep time. The crew sing as they row into battle.

THREE BANKS OF OARS

Trireme (in Greek *trieres*) means a 'three-oar' ship. The rowers were seated on staggered benches at three levels. Each oar was 4m to 4.2m in length.

> The Delphic oracle predicted Athens would be saved by its 'wooden walls'. The Athenians said that this meant its ships.

SEND IN THE MARINES

On the twin runways of the deck there was a group of up to 20 marines, or *epibatai*, including archers and armed hoplites for boarding enemy ships. The working crew of sailors numbered about 15.

MUSCLE POWER

Each ship needed 170 rowers, one to each oar. They were not slaves, but professional sailors, mostly from poorer households. The top speed was about 8 knots (15km/h).

BATTLE AT SALAMIS

After the battle of Thermopylae in 480BCE, the Persians were poised to conquer Greece. Athens was in flames. However, 21 western Greek city-states raised a fleet of 378 ships. The huge Persian fleet included Phoenicians, Egyptians and eastern Greeks, all from lands ruled by Persia. The western Greeks trapped the enemy in a channel by the island of Salamis. The battle lasted eight hours and 200 Persian ships were destroyed.

A trireme fatally rams an enemy ship so that it is holed at the waterline. Its rowers are thrown into the sea on impact.

Persian fleet

Athenian ships

"IMMEDIATELY SHIP STRUCK INTO SHIP ITS BRONZE-TIPPED PROW."
Aeschylus (c. 525–456BCE)
Greek dramatist, who served at Salamis, describes the battle in his play The Persians *(472BCE)*

The ram is a strong timber beam plated with bronze. It smashes into enemy ships.

ORACLE – a shrine where people could consult the gods about the future

Hephaestus
*god of fire,
blacksmiths and forges*

Aphrodite
*goddess of love
and beauty, whose
symbol was a dove*

Dionysus
*god of wine and drama,
who was worshipped
at wild festivals*

Ares
*god of war and
a bloodthirsty warrior,
whose father was Zeus*

Hera
*wife of Zeus and queen
of the gods, who was also
the goddess of marriage*

Poseidon
*god of the sea,
earthquakes and horses,
often shown holding a trident*

GODS OF OLYMPUS

Early Greek stories told how the universe was created from chaos. Out of this the first gods and goddesses came into being, representing the earth, the sea, the sky, and night and day. The Greeks had tales about many other gods as well. These represented human feelings such as love, forces of nature such as earthquakes, or human activities such as farming or fighting. Stories of giants, monsters, spirits and heroes were also told.

peaks of
Mount Olympus

POWER AND FATE

The most important gods and goddesses were said to live at the snowy summit of Greece's highest mountain, Olympus. They were ruled by Zeus, god of the sky, and were like humans, forever quarrelling amongst themselves. The gods and goddesses controlled the fate of human beings – they punished them, rewarded them, bewitched them and sometimes even fell in love with them.

"THEN WE WENT TO THE GOD'S PRECINCT, AND THERE ON THE ALTAR OUR CAKES AND OFFERINGS WERE DEDICATED, FOOD FOR HEPHAESTUS' FLAME."

Aristophanes (c. 448–388BCE)
Greek poet, from his play Wealth (c. 388BCE)

> One myth tells that Athena was so jealous of Arachne the weaver's skills that she turned her into a spider.

Artemis
moon goddess and a huntress with a bow and arrow

Hermes
messenger of the gods, who was worshipped by businessmen – and thieves!

Athena
patron goddess of Athens, victorious in battle and worshipped for her wisdom

Demeter
mother goddess representing fertility, farming and the seasons

Apollo
god of light, who was also linked with music, poetry and archery

Zeus
king of the gods, god of the sky, and the commander of thunder and lightning

⊜ THE ORACLE AT DELPHI

Delphi was a religious site on the slopes of Mount Parnassus. It was sacred to Apollo, who killed Python, a snake goddess who guarded the earth. Delphi was famous for its oracle. A priestess would go into a trance and speak the words of Apollo. Rulers and the famous would visit Delphi for guidance about their futures.

consulting the oracle (priestess is seated on the left)

TO THE TEMPLE

Greeks made offerings to the gods at their temples. Each year there would be a public procession to the temple in honour of a god or goddess, bringing an animal such as a sheep for sacrifice. At least one priest would have accompanied the procession on its journey.

DAILY LIFE

Older Greek towns grew up around a maze of streets and alleys. Later cities were better planned. Around the town you might see women with pottery jars fetching the daily water supply from street fountains or wells, slaves loading donkeys with supplies or children playing in the dust. The agora was the chief meeting place. This was where the men came to do business or talk politics, and where traders came to sell their goods.

AGORA – a district serving as the centre of public life in a Greek town

THE WOMEN'S ROOM

Women married when they were about 15 years old. They spent many hours each week spinning yarn and weaving cloth. In this room they might also play music, nurse their children or take their meals.

bedroom

kitchen

bathroom

⊖ GREEK CHILDHOOD

Many babies died at birth. Those who survived were given their name after a week or so. Athenian boys might be taught their father's trade, or go to school to learn reading, writing, sums, music and gymnastics. Girls might learn at home, studying reading, writing, music and weaving. At about 12, children were expected to give their toys to the gods, as a sign that they were grown up.

child taking toy to an altar, c. 425 BCE

ENSLAVED

There may have been as many slaves as free citizens in ancient Greece. They had to work as servants, nurses, cooks, labourers or miners. Some were born into slavery or sold as slaves when children. Others had been captured in wars.

> In Greece, a break-in was precisely that. Burglars could easily smash through the mud-brick walls.

Woollen blankets, clothes and wall hangings were woven on upright looms.

INSIDE THE HOME

Most homes were built of mud bricks and plaster, and had stone foundations and tiled roofs. Windows were small with wooden shutters. Wives managed the household and spent much of their time in the women's room. They had few rights, although in Sparta they could own property. Men led more public lives. Their room was used for business meetings or for entertaining friends.

www.ancientgreece.co.uk/dailylife/challenge/cha_set.html

women's room

slaves' quarters

men's room

Couches laid out for a symposium (a drinking and discussion party).

entrance hall

bedroom

playing knucklebones

courtyard

store room

juggling

workshop

THE COURTYARD

In the courtyard, slaves might be carrying in the shopping or sweeping up. Children would be playing or having lessons under a shady olive tree. Also, cooking or eating might take place here on sunny days.

PLAYTIME

Games included juggling (above) and knucklebones, in which five small bones or stones were tossed, caught and flipped on the hand. Small children played with dolls, toy animals, wheeled carts and yo-yos.

capital

pillar

Doric
*fluted (lined)
column with a plain,
simple capital*

Ionic
*capital (top)
is carved with a
graceful scroll*

CARVED COLUMNS

The Greeks were masters of arts and crafts, producing objects with technical skill and a sense of beauty. Magnificent public buildings and temples were supported by tall pillars, designed in various styles called 'orders'. Their tops, or capitals, were beautifully carved. Greek architecture, with its perfect proportions, would be imitated for thousands of years.

CREATING BEAUTY

Greek cities were noisy, industrious places. Around the agora, the central market, were busy workshops where smiths hammered iron and bronze, silversmiths made jewellery and stone workers chiselled blocks of marble. Potters produced fine vases, decorated at first with geometric patterns and later with figures of people or gods in black and red. Some goods were made on a large scale and exported around the Mediterranean.

⊖ THE POTTER'S CRAFT

Many Greek city-states had access to good clay. This sticky mud was used to make urns, vases, dishes, jugs and jars. These were generally shaped on a potter's wheel and fired (baked) in a kiln until hard. During the firing, the amount of air could be varied, which made the clay turn red. Areas painted with a coating, called a slip, remained black.

Geometrical ware
*patterned jug with
a decorative spout,
c. 675–650BCE*

Red figure ware
*shows a scene from
the Trojan War,
c. 480BCE*

Black figure ware
*cup featuring a bird-catcher
from Etruria (an area of
central Italy), c. 550BCE*

> Archaeologists have discovered that many marble statues were originally coloured with paints.

Corinthian
*slender column
is topped with ornate
stone leaves*

**Statues of women, called
caryatids, served as
pillars at the front of
some buildings.**

LIVING MARBLE

Greek sculptors worked in marble, bronze and clay.
The first statues looked rather stiff and unnatural.
After the 500s CE, the human body was shown in a
much more realistic way for the first time in history.

HOT METAL

Blacksmiths used furnaces to heat iron. They raised
the heat by puffing in air, using leather bellows. They
shaped the soft metal into tools and weapons. Other
specialists worked precious ornamental metals such as
gold, silver and electrum (a mixture of the two metals).

"BEAUTY IS TRUTH, TRUTH BEAUTY."
John Keats (1795–1821)
English poet, from his poem Ode on a Grecian Urn (1819)

HAIR FASHION

Greek women had long, flowing locks. In Sparta these were tied back in a ponytail, but in Athens the hair was braided into a bun with ribbons. Later fashions tucked curled hair into bands, nets and beautiful headdresses. Wigs and hair extensions were popular.

RIBBONS AND ROBES

Most Greek clothes were beautiful, but simple. They were woven on looms at home and were usually made from high-quality wool or linen. White cloth was popular, but bold colours could also be produced using natural dyes made from plants, insects and shellfish. By the 400s BCE, expensive silks and cottons were being imported from China and India.

The tunic falls in natural folds.

THE LOOK

Mirrors were made of polished bronze. What did they reflect? Rich women used make-up such as eye-liner and blusher, and powder to make the face pale. They did not want to look like poor women, who became sunburned working in the fields.

DRAPES AND FOLDS

This woman wears a peplos tunic. She has draped an outer wrap from her shoulder pin around her hips. Outer wraps were called himatia and could also be worn to veil the head or act as a cloak.

> Face powder was made from lead and was, in fact, poisonous.

WHAT TO WEAR

Greek dress was based on a tunic design, made from a single piece of cloth. Tunics were knee-length for working people or slaves, and ankle-length for wealthier citizens. The classic dress for women was a peplos – a sleeveless tunic with a high belt. It was pinned at each shoulder. Various styles of chiton also came into fashion. These were lighter, looser tunics, often with sleeves. Men also wore a simple version of the chiton.

To keep cool, the himation is draped low.

necklace c. 450BCE

earrings c. 850BCE

gold ring c. 450BCE

MENSWEAR

This man wears no under-tunic or chiton, just a large wrap or himation. This was much like the toga worn by Roman men. Men would often wear no clothes at all for exercise, athletics or military training.

GLEAMING GOLD

Gold, silver, ivory and precious stones were made into beautiful earrings, headdresses, pendants, necklaces and rings. These were often costly gifts and brought out only on special occasions. Rings were sometimes worn as lucky charms or in honour of the gods.

⊖ OUT AND ABOUT

Greeks often went barefoot, especially in the home. The normal footwear was a pair of sandals made of leather thongs. Short or high boots could be worn for riding or working outdoors. During hot Mediterranean summers, a broad, brimmed straw hat was ideal. On cooler, more wintry days, a cap or a fur hat might be needed, as well as a warm, woollen cloak.

brimmed hat

leather sandal

high boot

PHALANX – a battle formation perfected by the Macedonians

THE MARCH INTO ASIA

In 334BCE, Alexander crossed into Asia with an army of 30,000 foot soldiers and 5,000 cavalry. Ahead lay the troops of Darius III, emperor of Persia. Alexander's men fought their way across Asia Minor and conquered the lands known today as Syria, Lebanon, Egypt, Iraq, Iran, parts of Central Asia and Afghanistan. Darius suffered bitter defeats at the Granicus river, at Issus and Gaugamela. Alexander was victorious.

"O MY SON... MACEDONIA IS TOO SMALL FOR YOU."

King Philip II (382–336BCE)
said to his young son Alexander, as reported by the Greek historian Plutarch (c. 46–120CE)

ALEXANDER THE GREAT

King Alexander III was born in Pella, Macedonia, in 356BCE. As a boy, his tutor was the great philosopher Aristotle. In his short life, Alexander ('the Great') proved himself to be a brilliant general. He conquered one of the greatest empires the world had ever seen.

INDIAN WARFARE

In 326BCE, Alexander reached the Hydaspes river – known today as the Jhelum, in Pakistan. He defeated an Indian army under King Puruvura, who had 200 war elephants in his army.

THE AGE OF ALEXANDER

Macedonia was a kingdom on the northern borders of Greece. It became very powerful under the rule of a king called Philip II. In 338BCE, Philip defeated an alliance of city-states, including Athens and Thebes, at the battle of Chaeronea. He was murdered two years later. His son Alexander became king. Alexander put down rebellions and planned a war of all the Greeks against the old enemy, Persia.

DARIUS AT ISSUS

This mosaic picture, made in Italy in about 100BCE, shows Alexander (below, left) fighting Darius (below), probably at the battle of Issus in 333BCE. Darius was killed by his own men in 330BCE. Alexander gave him a fine funeral.

DEATH IN BABYLON

By 323BCE, Alexander was in Babylon, in what is now Iraq. After a feast in the royal palace, he suffered a severe fever. Some people believed he had caught a disease, such as malaria. Others thought he was poisoned by jealous rivals. He died aged only 32.

coins from the time of Alexander the Great

www.bbc.co.uk/history/historic_figures/alexander_the_great.shtml

☻ THE FEARSOME PHALANX

The phalanx was a terrifying battle formation made up of a great block of fighting men with spears. The Spartans used short spears, but the Macedonians used huge spears called sarissas that were up to 6.5m long. The front ranks pointed them forwards. The rear held them up at angles to break the flights of arrows.

Macedonian phalanx in battle order

THE OLYMPIC GAMES

"LIVE BY RULE, SUBMIT TO DIET...
EXERCISE YOUR BODY AT STATED
HOURS, IN HEAT OR IN COLD..."

Epictetus (55–135CE)
*philosopher, his words on training for the Olympics,
from **The Enchiridion** (135CE)*

Thrilling athletic contests, or games, were held in Delphi, Nemea, Corinth and Olympia that were open to athletes from all over the Greek world. The games began as a kind of religious festival, held in honour of the gods. The Olympic Games are believed to have started in 776BCE and were celebrated every four years until 393CE. They were revived as an international competition in 1896 and have become the biggest sporting event of the modern world.

statue of Zeus as Horkios, taker of oaths, with a lightning bolt in each hand

RUNNING FOR ZEUS

During the Olympic Games, city-states had to stop fighting one another. Nobody travelling to the games could be harmed, for they were under the special protection of the gods. Athletes and officials joined a two-day procession from Elis to Olympia – a valley in the south-west of Greece – where there was a great temple dedicated to Zeus. There they were welcomed by an excited crowd. The Olympic site included other temples, tracks, racecourses, hostels and restaurants.

TOP EVENTS

The footrace was originally the most important event in the games. The first known Olympic champion was Coroebus, a baker from Elis, in 776BCE. Javelin, discus (left), running and long jump were not separate events, but part of the pentathlon, which was decided by a wrestling match between the top two athletes.

Boars are sacrificed to Zeus, king of the gods.

> Women held their own separate games at Olympia, in honour of the goddess Hera.

THRILLS AND SPILLS

More sports were added to the games, including boxing, running in armour, all-in combat and horseracing. One of the most popular events was chariot racing, with teams of two or four horses. The action was fast and furious, and very dangerous for the charioteer.

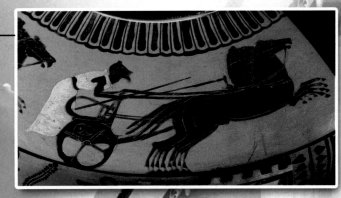

The games begin with a swearing-in ceremony at the council chamber.

THE CHAMPIONS

At the end of the games, the winners were summoned to the Temple of Zeus. They were not given medals, but were crowned by the judges with a wreath of olive leaves. Finally, a great feast was held in their honour.

FAIR PLAY

Athletes were not supposed to be paid, but a winner could expect to be showered with gifts when he returned to his home city. Sometimes, there were political rows and accusations of foul play. Fines imposed on cheats were used to pay for new statues of Zeus at Olympia.

Athletes, holding portions of the sacrifice, swear to obey the rules.

Athletes, their families and trainers, and Olympic officials all queue to take the oath to Zeus.

GREEK LEGACY

Many different lands shaped the civilizations of ancient Greece, from Europe to western Asia and Egypt. Classical Greece provided the foundations for a new European culture, with its great achievements in philosophy, politics, mathematics, architecture, drama and music. Even today, European languages are full of words that come from ancient Greek. Ideas from that distant period of history have spread around the modern world.

GREEKS AND ROMANS

The first part of this memorial is written in the Greek language and letters. The second part is in Latin, the language of Rome. Many Romans could speak Greek, and the two Mediterranean peoples shared similar beliefs and customs.

THE BYZANTINES

In 667BCE, the Greeks founded a colony named Byzantium. In 330CE, the Romans built a fine new city on the site, calling it Constantinople (now named Istanbul). It became the eastern capital of the Roman empire, thriving long after Rome had lost power, and became the centre of a Christian 'Byzantine' empire. Constantinople was captured by Muslim Turks in 1453. Greece won independence from Turkish rule in 1832.

The splendid Christian Church of Holy Wisdom was completed in 537CE. It later became a Muslim mosque and it has been a museum since 1935.

Hagia Sophia, Istanbul

> The modern Greek language is spoken by about 11 million people in Greece and by a further two million worldwide.

JUSTINIAN THE GREAT

Justinian I was emperor from 527 to 565CE. He set about winning back the lands of the western Roman empire. In his own eastern empire, Roman law was still used, but people spoke Greek and its 'Orthodox' forms of Christian worship developed separately from those of Rome.

The minarets (prayer towers) date from the building's period as a Turkish mosque.

⊖ THE GREAT REVIVAL

Many ancient Greek ideas were respected by Christians in the Middle Ages. Precious records of their work were protected by scholars in the Muslim world. In the 1400s and 1500s, there was a great revival or 'Renaissance' of interest in ancient Greece and Rome. Greek and Latin were taught in schools. Discoveries of sites such as Mycenae and Knossos fascinated new generations in the 1800s and 1900s.

Plato and Aristotle feature in this 1510–11 painting by Raphael, an artist of the Italian Renaissance.

http://byzantium.seashell.net.nz/articlemain.php?artid=mapbase_565

DEMOKRATÍA

The modern Greek parliament meets in Athens, where the idea of democracy was born more than 2,500 years ago. Modern governments may view democracy in many different ways, but most still claim that rule by the people is central to their ideals as a nation.

INVESTIGATE

The world of ancient Greece may not be as far away as you think –
just look in a museum, in a book, or on the stage or screen.

MUSEUMS AND EXHIBITIONS

In most countries in Europe and in many British cities you will find
museums showing beautiful Greek pottery, statues, coins or jewellery.

The Pocket Timeline of Ancient Greece by Emma McAllister
(British Museum Press)

Ashmolean Museum of Art and Archaeology,
Beaumont Street, Oxford, OX1 2PH, UK

**ruins of the Temple of
Poseidon, Sounion, Greece**

www.ashmolean.org

**clay tablet showing
a woman at a table
from Locris, Greece**

ARCHAEOLOGY

If you are interested in archaeology, make a start by joining a local
group for young people. If you go on holiday to Greece, Turkey or
southern Italy, you can even visit the ancient Greek sites for yourself.

Greece by Stephen Biesty (Oxford University Press)

Palace of Knossos, near Heraklion, Crete

**scene from a film about
Alexander the Great**

www.yac-uk.org

FICTION, STAGE AND SCREEN

Myths, legends and tales of ancient Greece have always inspired writers
and film-makers, and they can recreate the ancient magic just for you.
Why not make Greek masks or put on a Greek drama at your school?

**writings of the
ancient Greek
historian Herodotus
can be read today**

Black Ships Before Troy by Rosemary Sutcliffe
(Frances Lincoln)

Hercules DVD (Walt Disney Home Video)

www.greektheatre.gr

RESEARCH

A visit to your local library is sure to offer information on ancient Greece.
To see hoplites in action, check out re-enactment performances near you.

The Usborne Encyclopedia of Ancient Greece by Jane Chisholm (Usborne)

British Museum, Great Russell Street, London, WC1B 3DG, UK

www.hoplites.org/index.htm

ANCIENT
ROME

Samnite cavalry

Samnite infantry

Crests make the warrior look taller and scarier.

A breastplate is worn over a tunic.

This Samnite carries a round shield in the Greek style.

ROMAN REPUBLIC

The Romans fought their way to power, defeating other peoples living in Italy. They battled amongst themselves, too. In 510BCE they overthrew their king and Rome became a republic, governed by the Senate and popular assemblies which elected Rome's magistrates, including two consuls, or leaders. Patricians (noblemen) were still powerful. Ordinary citizens, called plebeians, had to struggle for their rights.

S.P.Q.R.

Roman government was carried out in the name of the people. The initial letters S.P.Q.R. on items such as this battle standard stood for **S**enatus **P**opulus**q**ue **R**omanus – meaning 'the Senate and the People of Rome'.

WARRING NEIGHBOURS

The Samnites were warriors, originally from the hills of southern Italy, who fought the Romans during three fierce wars between 343 and 290BCE. By about 250BCE, Rome had gained control over most of Italy, either by treaty or by military force.

> The Romans built the first paved roads across Italy to allow their armies to move quickly, so they could fight the Samnites.

A pommel balances the blade of the sword (gladius).

Plates (bucculae) protect the cheeks.

The first Roman soldiers were property-owning citizens who provided their own armour.

The pilum (spear) could pierce enemy armour.

LOYAL SOLDIERS

At first, Roman soldiers were recruited for one campaign at a time. After 107BCE, the army became a professional, long-term fighting force. The Republican period was later known for its strong sense of duty and stern discipline.

Roman helmet (galea)

short sword (gladius)

⊖ SAVED BY GEESE

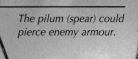

In 390BCE Rome was attacked. The Gauls, a Celtic people, burned and looted much of the city, while the Romans took refuge on the Capitoline Hill. It was said that the Romans were alerted to the enemy's arrival when sacred geese, kept on the hill, began to cackle loudly.

TAXATION – money collected from the public for use by the government

ROMAN WORLD

The Roman empire at its largest stretched from the coast of what is now Portugal to Iraq, from the Scottish borders to Morocco, from Romania to Egypt. Along its dusty roads tramped the legions, enforcing Roman rule. On its rivers and seas sailed merchant ships, trading in grain, oil, wine, olives, marble, metals, glass, pottery, textiles – and slaves. This vast area used the same currency, with coins of bronze, silver and gold.

NORTHERN LANDS

Roman-occupied Britain (Britannia) exported woollen cloaks, hunting dogs, lead and silver.

The Roman empire spanned snowy moorlands, fertile river valleys and hot deserts (right).

RIVER DANUBE

The Danube, stretching from Germany to the Black Sea, formed an important border, and forts were built along it.

☻ MADE IN THE EMPIRE

The Romans were great craft workers, and also learned new skills from peoples they conquered. They imported glass from western Asia and Egypt. Pottery was made in Italy and in Gaul, where red pottery dishes known as 'Samian ware' were produced for export. Roman goldsmiths crafted fine jewellery, inlaid with precious stones.

gold 'snake' armband

glass jug

> About 56 million people lived within the Roman empire by the 300s CE.

Wine and olive oil were transported and stored in amphorae (pottery jars with handles). They are sometimes brought to light when Roman shipwrecks are discovered.

SOUTH TO EGYPT

Egypt's civilization was already thousands of years old when it became part of the Roman empire in 30BCE. The Romans profited from taxation and from the grain grown in the Nile valley.

Roman tourists came to marvel at ancient Egyptian monuments, such as the Pyramids of Giza.

mosaics showing merchant ships from Ostia, the ancient port of Rome

LUSH VINEYARDS

The Romans were expert growers of the grape vine. They brought their skills from Italy to many parts of the empire, and often planted vineyards on sunny hillsides.

TRADING ROUTES

Trading routes extended overland through Asia and Africa. They connected with seaports around the Mediterranean and the Black Sea. A sea voyage from southern Spain to Italy took about nine days, while Egypt to Italy could take about 15.

"GLORIA EXERCITUS"
(GLORY TO THE ARMY)

wording on many Roman coins

Dacians fought with swords, battle scythes, spears, bows and arrows.

signum
(battle standard)

BATTLE HONOURS

Dacians fight like cornered wolves as Roman legions steadily advance. Dacia was the part of eastern Europe now known as Romania and Moldova. In 85–86, 101–102 and 105–106CE it was repeatedly ravaged by war. Rome was victorious, winning control of the region's rich gold mines. Thousands of Dacians were sent back to Rome as slaves.

Dacian warrior

> In 9CE three whole Roman legions were defeated and destroyed in a single battle in Germany.

LEGIONS AT WAR

The Roman army, ruthless, well-trained and disciplined, seemed unstoppable. It was usually divided into fighting units called legions, each made up of some 5,500 men. Legions were supported by cavalry and non-Roman troops called auxiliaries. A soldier's life was tough. He might have to march over 30km a day, carrying tools and food as well as sword, shield and spears.

STORY IN STONE

Trajan's Column in Rome dates from 113CE. It pictures scenes from Roman victories in the Dacian wars. From these we can learn about details of Roman armour, hand weapons, catapults, bridge building, forts and ships.

A fighting unit of about 80 soldiers was called a century.

Roman reserves wait to join the battle.

Segmented armour is made up of metal plates.

scutum (shield)

LEG·X·GEM

www.caerleon.net/history/army/page2.html

HAIL, CAESAR!

Gaius Julius Caesar (100–44BCE) was a brilliant general. He conquered Gaul, invaded Britain and fought right across the Roman empire. He defeated his rivals in bitter civil wars. Military success brought him popularity and great political power, but this proved to be his undoing. Caesar's enemies complained that no single man should hold so much power in a republic. They plotted against him.

GAULS – Celtic tribes living in modern-day France, Belgium and the Alps

LEG XII

Caesar surrounded Alesia with a double circle of timber walls and towers.

The relief army of Gauls lies dead, or is carried off into slavery.

Vercingetorix lays down his sword and shield in surrender to Caesar. He was taken to Rome in chains and executed in 46BCE.

> Julius Caesar was captured by pirates in 75BCE. Once freed, he had them all executed.

CONQUEROR OF ALL

In this scene, Julius Caesar accepts the surrender of Vercingetorix, commander of the Gauls, at Alesia in 52BCE. The fort has been besieged, trapped within an iron ring of Roman troops. A huge army of Gauls has been slaughtered trying to break the siege. After a six-year campaign, heavily resisted by the Gauls, Caesar has finally won this province and all its riches for Rome.

THE HISTORY MAKER

Julius Caesar came from a noble family, which claimed descent from Aeneas himself. His life changed Roman history. His death was followed by civil war, and prepared the way for Rome to be ruled by emperors.

People from the fort are rounded up as prisoners, and disarmed.

www.livius.org/caa-can/caesar/caesar00.html

LEG VII

⊖ THE DOWNFALL

Would Julius Caesar become king? Republicans were enraged by the idea of anyone becoming this powerful. On 15 March 44BCE a group of conspirators, led by Marcus Junius Brutus and Gaius Cassius Longinus, attacked him in Rome. He died from 23 stab wounds.

a coin marking the assassination of Caesar (Brutus on one side, daggers on the other)

The channel runs slightly downhill so that the water flows easily.

This section of the channel is enclosed, for the water. It will be lined with cement.

THE AQUEDUCT

Labourers haul, heave and sweat. Masons chip at great blocks of stone. Carpenters build timber frames and scaffolding. The new aqueduct will carry a supply of spring water from the hills to a nearby city. High arches are needed to support the aqueduct as it crosses a river valley.

Slaves clear rubble on the building site.

BUILDING IN STONE

The Romans were a practical people. The success of their empire depended on technology and engineering, on roads, bridges, dams, drains, mines, millstones and cranes. They learned how to build stone arches from the Etruscans, and how to build waterwheels from the Greeks and Asians. Their own brilliant invention was Roman concrete, made from a special type of cement.

> Roman cranes were often powered by treadwheels, turned by tramping slaves.

STAYING POWER

This fine Roman aqueduct is the Pont du Gard in southern France. It is 49m high and 275m long. It has survived nearly 2,000 years. Hundreds of other examples of Roman engineering can still be seen throughout the old empire.

⊖ ALL ROADS LEAD TO ROME

The Romans built long, straight highways from place to place. Routes were carefully surveyed and the roads were well paved and drained, and built on firm foundations. The road network provided fast communications across the empire, encouraged trade and allowed the rapid movement of troops.

paving stones on the Appian Way, Rome's most important road

Cranes with treadwheels could lift much heavier loads than cranes with winches.

The piers rise from rock in the river bed.

The Roman empire in 117 CE

RISE OF THE EMPIRE

The murder of Julius Caesar did not mark a return to republican government after all. After years of strife, it was Caesar's great-nephew (and adopted son), Octavian, who came to rule Rome in 27 BCE. His new title was Imperator Caesar Augustus. Augustus did not abolish the republic, but simply took over more and more public offices for himself. Soon the Senate was losing any real power. Rome's future belonged to its emperors.

EMPIRE – many different lands ruled by a single government or emperor

RULING FROM ROME

Rome was becoming the hub of a great empire. What happened there affected not only people in Italy, but Britons, Gauls, Germans, Greeks, Phoenicians, Iberians, Africans and Asians. Rome even made contact with the emperors of China.

KEY

1. Circus Maximus, a racecourse
2. the Roman Forum
3. Imperial Palace
4. Aqua Claudia aqueduct
5. Flavian amphitheatre (Colosseum)
6. Temple of the Divine Claudius
7. Baths of Trajan

> More than a billion (1,000,000,000) litres of water had to be channelled into Rome each day.

THE COLOUR OF POWER

A type of sea snail called the murex provided a reddish-purple dye, which was first traded by the Phoenicians. The dye was very expensive, so the colour became a symbol of royalty or nobility in the ancient world. In Rome, the colour purple was reserved for emperors.

murex shell

"HE COULD BOAST THAT HE INHERITED IT BRICK AND LEFT IT MARBLE."

Suetonius (c. 69–c. 130CE)
Roman historian, describing Emperor Augustus's improvements to Rome

http://resourcesforhistory.com/map.htm

A SPLENDID CITY

Every emperor wanted to leave his mark on Rome in the form of fine new public buildings, gleaming with marble. To a slave arriving from northern Europe, the sight must have been incredible. The capital had racecourses, temples, theatres, law courts, public baths, busy markets and grand palaces.

CITY STREETS

Roman cities were surrounded by walls, and had public gates and paved roads for the traffic going in and out. In Rome itself and in other big cities there were large apartment blocks, called insulae, as well as town houses large and small. These had only small shuttered windows and wooden doors facing the street. Streets were noisy with the cries of shopkeepers, market traders and rumbling cartwheels.

STROLL BACK IN TIME

You can wander today through the streets of Pompeii and Herculaneum, near Naples, Italy. These towns were buried by the eruption of Vesuvius in 79CE. There, it is easy to imagine how the Romans lived, traded and entertained themselves.

The latest shipment of slaves goes on sale.

ROMAN SLAVES

Around one-third of the population may have been slaves. Brought from all over the empire, slaves were owned by their master, could be bought and sold, and had no rights. Some worked as household servants, tutors, labourers or miners. They might be freed as a reward for good service.

This tag, worn by a slave, asks the public to return him to his owner if he runs away.

A Greek tutor takes his pupils to class.

busy market stalls

Augustus set up a body of firefighters and watchmen to protect Rome.

www.vroma.org/~bmcmanus/house.html

A CITY CORNER

This corner of the city, a little way from the centre, is linked by main road to the forum, which is where the public buildings, temples and central markets are located. Here the morning's activities are getting under way. Shops are open. A wealthy patrician talks with his wife in his garden, while his daughter is carried by litter to visit relatives.

shop selling hot food

stepping stones

A thief runs off with some fruit.

patrician's courtyard garden

shop selling cloth

ANCIENT RELIGION

Throughout the year, Romans took part in festivals, sacrifices and religious rituals. Their religion developed out of a belief in spirits of the countryside and the home. It also took ideas of gods and goddesses from the Etruscans and from Greek settlers in Italy. The Romans made offerings and prayers to many different gods, and expected personal protection and favours in return.

Wine or incense would be offered at this shrine, called a lararium.

ROMAN TEMPLES

Splendid temples were built all over the empire, often by emperors or generals as thanksgiving for victory. Temples were centres of sacrifice and ritual. People did not go inside them to worship together.

a Roman temple in Syria

HOUSEHOLD GODS

Special gods looked after the home, the hearth and kitchen, as well as weddings and funerals. They were known as Lares and Penates. Each household had one Lar and two Penates, with their own shrines.

⊖ GODS OF THE ROMAN STATE

Many gods and goddesses were officially worshipped as protectors of Roman cities, or of the state. In later days, the emperor served as high priest. Jupiter, Juno and Minerva were the chief gods and goddesses honoured in Rome.

Diana (left) was a goddess of woodland and hunting, and was also associated with the moon. She was the daughter of Jupiter.

Jupiter (left) was the greatest of the gods, a force of light, of thunder and lightning, and chief protector of the state.

Mars (left), originally a god of farming, was worshipped as the god of war. He was the father of Romulus and Remus.

Mercury (right) was the god of merchants and commerce, and was the messenger of the gods. He wore winged shoes.

> Roman priests tried to find out the intentions of the gods by studying the flight of birds.

SACRIFICE OF A BULL

Important events and festivals were marked by sacrifices. Animals were killed as offerings, to please the gods and so prevent disasters. The choice of animal, the way it was killed and the examination of its intestines were very precise rituals. One mistake, and another sacrifice would have to be carried out in its place.

KEY

1 priest carrying an offering of wine

2 altar, where organs of the sacred animal were burned

3 flamen, the senior priest, wearing a conical hat and laurel wreath

4 attendant, carrying the hammer used to kill the bull

5 haruspex, the priest who will inspect the bull's entrails

6 bull – a white bull was sacrificed to Jupiter or Mars

7 attendant catching the bull's blood

AMPHITHEATRE – *a circular or oval stadium – the word means 'double-theatre'*

STAGE AND ARENA

Roman entertainment included music, singing, dance and theatre. Romans also loved to play dice and watch horse races or boxing. Then, in amphitheatres such as Rome's Colosseum, there were gladiator fights: violent shows where packed crowds watched trained combatants fight, sometimes to the death.

DIE, GLADIATOR!

Gladiators were divided into various types, according to their armour, helmet or the weapons they used. They fought one pair at a time, and each type usually fought another particular type, although this scene imagines several fighting at once. The bravest gladiators were very popular with the crowds, and could win a lot of prize money.

retarius

Thracian

ACTING A PART

Romans took their ideas about drama from the Greeks. Comedies were very popular. Actors wore masks to represent the characters they played. Dramas were staged in large open-air theatres.

> In 107CE 5,000 pairs of gladiators took part in the biggest ever session of combat.

SPQR

murmillo

A greave (ocrea) protected the leg.

The name 'gladiator' means swordsman.

Arena was the Latin word for sand. The combat area was filled with sand to soak up the blood. It was freshly raked after each contest.

secutor

Many gladiators met an early death in the arena.

⊖ THRILLS AND SPILLS AT THE RACES

four-horse chariot (quadriga)

The Circus Maximus was Rome's great race track, and could seat over 150,000 spectators. Here people could place their bets, watch chariots thunder around the track and cheer on their team (Reds, Greens, Blues or Whites). They watched jockeys risk their lives by jumping from horse to horse or leaping over chariots.

FASHION AND STYLE

All Roman clothes were based on the simple tunic. Slaves and working people wore a cheap, practical version of this garment. A wealthy Roman citizen would wear a short linen tunic beneath a long robe called a toga. The ladies of his family would wear an under-tunic with a long, high-waisted over-tunic or dress called a stola. Sometimes they would cover this with a shawl, called a palla, draped over their shoulders or head.

TOGA – a heavy woollen robe, cut in a semi-circle, folded and draped over the body

By the 2nd century CE, rich women's hair styles had become very elaborate. Many women curled and bleached their hair. Some wore hair extensions or wigs.

The glitter of gold and the sheen of mother-of-pearl made this necklace a desirable item in first-century Pompeii.

LUCKY LOCKET

The bulla might be made of leather, cloth or gold.

Each Roman child was given a locket at birth. Called a bulla, it was worn around the neck at all times. It contained an amulet or good-luck charm, and was worn until the child was grown-up (for girls, this was when they married).

make-up casket

Venus, goddess of love, makes herself beautiful.

CHANGING CLOTH

Women enjoyed different colours and styles, and liked to keep up with changes in the fabrics available: moving from wool to linen or cotton, and later even to expensive imported silk. Men's woollen togas were often too bulky for comfort. After about 100CE they became smaller and more lightweight.

PREPARING FOR A PARTY

A wealthy woman would spend hours getting ready for a party. Her slaves would bring mirrors, hairpins, perfumes and oils. Cosmetics included pale face-powder made from chalk or (poisonous) lead, and lipstick made from red ochre.

> One emperor even got his nickname because as a child he wore a certain style of boots: Caligula means 'little army boots'.

THE PURPLE STRIPE

a leading citizen

Dress showed a person's rank in society. Any free-born Roman citizen could wear a plain white toga, although he might not do so every day. Boys under the age of 16 wore the toga with a purple stripe, and important people also wore a stripe as adults. A broad purple stripe was worn by senators only.

A traveller wears a practical woollen cloak.

WARM AND DRY

Woollen cloaks and capes, often with hoods, were worn by men and women to keep warm and stay dry. Farm workers in muddy fields might also bind their legs with strips of cloth, and soldiers wore breeches under their tunics.

STEPPING OUT

Skilled cobblers made footwear for all purposes. Romans wore light leather sandals indoors, and stouter shoes or sandals outdoors. Calf-length boots might be worn by huntsmen or army officers. Military footwear had studded soles.

a Roman woman wearing a stola and her husband wearing a tunic and everyday toga

GERMANIC – *belonging to a group of northern European peoples, including Angles, Saxons, Franks, Vandals and Goths*

ROME LIVES ON

> "WHILE STANDS THE COLOSSEUM, ROME SHALL STAND; WHEN FALLS THE COLOSSEUM, ROME SHALL FALL; AND WHEN ROME FALLS – THE WORLD."
>
> **Lord Byron (1788–1824)**
> *English poet, in the poem Childe Harold's Pilgrimage*

The Byzantine emperors failed to hold on to Rome's lands in the west. Much of the old empire came under the rule of Germanic kings. One of these, the Frankish ruler Charlemagne, created a new 'Holy Roman empire' in 800. The city of Rome remained the headquarters of the Catholic church. This ensured that it kept great political power and influence for hundreds of years.

Medieval scriptures (church writings) were copied in Latin.

THE ROMAN CHURCH

The Roman Catholic church dominated the lives of people in western Europe throughout the Middle Ages. The church used the Romans' language. Official documents were in Latin, and scholars wrote and studied in Latin. For centuries afterwards, scientists and scholars wrote in Latin rather than their own languages.

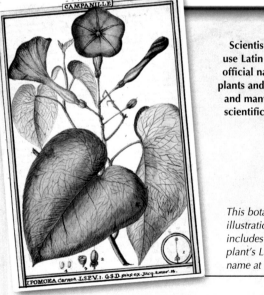

CAMPANILLE

IPOMOEA Carnea L.S.P.V.I. G.S.D. pinx ex. Jacq.amer. tb.

This botanical illustration includes the plant's Latin name at its base.

Scientists still use Latin for the official names of plants and animals and many other scientific terms.

> Catalan, French, Italian, Spanish, Portuguese and Romanian are just some of the languages descended from Latin.

⊖ ROME ALL AROUND US

The Roman style of architecture, which includes buildings with tall columns or impressive domes, became very popular again in Europe from about the 16th century onwards. Many grand public buildings are built in the Roman or 'neoclassical' style. Modern legal systems, too, have been influenced by the laws of the Roman and Byzantine empires. Many parliaments are still called 'Senate', like that of ancient Rome. Thousands of years after Rome was founded, it still affects our daily lives.

the Parliament of the European Union, which reunites many of the old parts of the Roman empire

The US Capitol in Washington D.C. includes the Senate and the House of Representatives. It is built in a neoclassical style.

NEW EMPERORS

During the French Revolution (1789–1799) many people took Republican Rome as their ideal. When Napoleon became emperor of France in 1804, he adopted symbols of the Roman empire, such as wreaths and eagles.

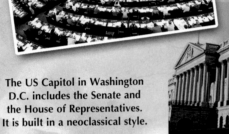

ANCIENT ROME TODAY

Tourists admire the Colosseum in Rome, and imagine the gladiators fighting and the roar of the crowd. All over the old empire there are fascinating reminders of the past, from forts and temples to public baths and aqueducts.

The heart of ancient Rome is recreated for television.

BRINGING ROME BACK TO LIFE

Mobile telephones and sound recording equipment? Can this be ancient Rome? Actors take a break between filming scenes from *Rome*. This successful television series was shot in Italy – much of it in Rome itself – in 2005–2007. Films, television programmes and novels all ensure that the Roman age is kept alive in our imagination.

INVESTIGATE

Get in touch with the past by visiting archaeological sites or museums. Read some ancient Roman writers (in English), or cook a Roman meal!

the Roman baths and museum at Bath, England

MUSEUMS AND EXHIBITIONS

All over Great Britain there are local museums with real Roman coins, weapons and statues. These help you to imagine what it was like to be a Roman soldier or a slave.

The British Museum Pocket Timeline of Ancient Rome (British Museum Press)

The Roman Baths at Bath, Abbey Church Yard, Bath BA1 1LZ, UK

www.britishmuseum.org

a wall-painting excavated in Pompeii, Italy

ARCHAEOLOGY

Roman forts, amphitheatres, baths, villas and temples can be visited at home or abroad. Many archaeological finds from excavations at Roman sites tell us fascinating details of everyday life in ancient times.

Pompeii by Richard Platt and Manuela Cappon (Kingfisher)

The Museum of London, London Wall, London EC2Y 5HN, UK

www.yac-uk.org and www.channel4.com/programmes/time-team

the character of Flavia in the Children's BBC TV adaptation of the Roman Mysteries books

ART AND FICTION

Novels set in Rome are always popular, and Roman mythology has some great stories, too. If you are interested in art, original mosaics and wall paintings have survived and can be seen at some museums.

The Orchard Book of Roman Myths by Geraldine McCaughrean and Emma Chichester Clark (Orchard)

The Roman Painted House at Dover, New Street, Dover, Kent CT17 9AJ, UK

www.romanmysteries.com

ruins of the Roman Library of Celsus in Ephesus, Turkey

ROMAN BUILDINGS

Find out about old Roman buildings near you. What were they made of? How were they different from Roman buildings in Rome itself, or other parts of the empire?

Rome in Spectacular Cross-section by Stephen Biesty (Oxford University Press)

Fishbourne Roman palace, Salthill Road, Fishbourne, Chichester, West Sussex, PO19 3QR, UK

www.vindolanda.com

GLOSSARY

agora
The central market and business district in a Greek town; the forum.

altar
A table or slab where offerings are made to a god or goddess.

amulet
A charm believed to offer magical protection against evil and danger.

archaeologist
A scientist who studies human history through archaeology – the excavation and analysis of objects and artefacts.

architect
Someone who designs and supervises the construction of buildings.

arena
The sand-covered area in a Roman amphitheatre where shows were staged.

assassinate
To murder a public figure, often for political reasons.

auxiliary
In a supporting role. Foreign auxiliary troops often fought alongside the Roman legions.

Books of the Dead
Spells written on papyrus and placed in Egyptian tombs from the New Kingdom to the Greco-Roman period.

bronze
A metal that is an alloy (mixture) of copper and tin, and used for making tools and weapons.

bulla
A lucky charm or amulet, worn around the neck by Roman children.

Byzantine Empire
The empire that grew out of the eastern division of the Roman empire.

canopic jar
A special container for storing the internal organs of a deceased person.

cavalry
Troops mounted on horseback.

Celts
A group of ancient European peoples, who by early Roman times were living in Britain, Ireland, France, Germany, Spain, northern Italy and Turkey.

chariot
A light cart, normally pulled by horses, used in warfare or sport.

city-state
A small, independent nation based on a single city and the surrounding region or island.

consul
One of the two joint leaders of the Roman republic, elected each year by an assembly of mostly wealthy and powerful Romans. Under the empire, consuls still existed but had no real power.

Dacians
An ancient people that in Roman times inhabited an area that is now mostly covered by Romania.

delta
A triangular area of land at the mouth of a large river where it divides into several smaller streams and flows into the sea.

democracy
Rule by the people, or by their representatives.

empire
A group of different countries, lands or peoples under the control of one ruler.

excavation
The site of a dig to uncover or unearth artefacts or remains from the past.

faience
Glazed pottery made by baking quartz sand with other minerals.

flax
A flowering plant cultivated for its fibres, which are spun into linen cloth.

forum
The centre of business, trade, government and religion in an ancient Roman town.

gladiator
A trained fighter who in Roman times engaged in mortal combat to entertain a crowd.

Goths
A group of Germanic tribes who invaded the lands of the Roman empire.

graffiti
Pictures or writings drawn or scratched on a wall or other surface.

hieroglyph
A symbol or small picture representing a word, sound or idea, used as the basis for the ancient Egyptian writing system.

hoplite
An ancient Greek footsoldier armed with a spear, sword and shield.

inundation
The annual flooding of the River Nile in Egypt during the summer.

irrigation
The process of bringing a flow of water to dry farmland, often by canals.

kohl
A black powder used as a cosmetic in Egypt to darken the rims of the eyelids.

Latin
The main language of the Roman empire.

legion
The basic fighting unit of the Roman army, containing around 5,000 soldiers.

litter
A platform used to carry wealthy passengers in Roman times.

mastaba
A type of Egyptian tomb in the Early Dynastic and Old Kingdom, which was rectangular with a flat roof.

Minoan
Belonging to the first great Greek civilization on the island of Crete, from about 2700 to 1420BCE.

mosaic
A picture made from small pieces of tile, pottery, stone or glass.

mummification
The embalming and drying of a body to prepare it for preservation and burial.

Mycenaean
Belonging to the civilization that grew around the citadels of southern Greece from about 1600 to 1100BCE.

natron
A moisture-absorbing salt used to dry a corpse during mummification.

Nubia
A country to the south of Egypt in the area of modern-day Sudan.

papyrus
A type of reed used to make boats, rope, baskets and paper in ancient Egypt.

patrician
A member of one of the ancient aristocratic families of Rome.

pharaoh
The title, meaning 'great house', given to the rulers of ancient Egypt.

plebeian
Belonging to an ordinary Roman family, rather than the upper, or patrician, class.

Ptolemaic
Of the dynastic house of the Ptolemies and their rule (305–30BCE), and the descendants of Alexander the Great's general, Ptolemy.

republic
A state ruled by the people or their representatives, rather than by a king, queen or emperor.

rituals
Formal actions that are performed in a particular, solemn way, often as part of religious worship or public ceremonies.

sacrifice
The act of offering something to a god, especially the ritual slaughter of an animal or human being.

sarissa
A very long spear used by Macedonian soldiers in battle.

scarab
A representation of a dung beetle, used by the ancient Egyptians as a symbol, seal, hieroglyph or amulet.

senate
The governing assembly of ancient Rome, chosen from leading citizens. It advised the consuls who could pass laws.

shabti
Model figures buried with important people in ancient Egypt so they could perform manual tasks as servants to the dead in the afterlife.

shrine
A holy place or temple.

siege
The surrounding of a city by an army, with the aim of cutting off its supplies and forcing it to surrender.

slave
Someone who has no freedom, and who is bought, sold and forced to work for no reward.

throwing stick
A wooden hunting tool, similar to a boomerang, used to injure or kill prey in ancient Egypt.

trident
A three-pronged spear.

trireme
A warship with three banks of rowers.

vizier
The highest official in the Egyptian government.

INDEX